P9-AQB-850

a northern alphabet

Dedicated to William Hamilton of Swan Hills, Alberta
and all the children north of sixty.

First printing
Published in Canada by
Tundra Books of Montreal
Montreal, Quebec   H3G 1R4
ISBN 0-88776-133-X

Published in the United States by
Tundra Books of Northern New York
Plattsburgh, N.Y. 12901
Library of Congress Catalog Card No. 82-050244

Distributed in Australia, New Zealand
and Southeast Asia by Childerset Pty.
Ltd., Melbourne, Australia.

Tundra Books has allocated a part of
its 1982 block grant from the Canada
Council toward the production of
this book.

Design by Dan O'Leary
Transparencies by A. Kilbertus
Typesetting by Compoplus, Montreal
Printed in Canada by Pierre Des Marais, Montreal

Arctic Beaver Cabin Drums Eagle Fire Geese Husky Igloo Jackrabbit Kayak Loon Muskeg North Owl Pack Quill

a northern alphabet

by Ted Harrison

Tundra Books

Raven Snow Trout Uniform Valley Walrus Xmas Yukon Zipper Alaska Bear Canada Dancers Ermine Forest Game

This is an alphabet book. But it is also a puzzle book, a story book and a games book.

The North is full of interest. The names of some of its people, places, animals and objects are mentioned under each letter. How many more can you find in the paintings? If you need some help, turn to the back of the book.

Every picture is also the beginning of a story. Can you make up the rest of the story to tell yourself and your friends?

And if you like to play games, see how many words—not just nouns, but also verbs, adjectives and adverbs—you can put into your story using the letter on the page. Take the letter T for instance. The story starts: Trapper Tom has three frozen trout. You might continue: He tripped over his toboggan as he was tramping through the snow to his trapline. What happened next?

Have fun.

Ted Harrison   Whitehorse, The Yukon

Aa

Alex lives
in the **Arctic.**
He is wearing an
anorak.

British Columbia   Baffin   Beaufort Sea   Bering Sea   Bathurst Inlet   Baker Lake   Boothia   Brooks Range   Black Tickle   British Mountains

Braeburn Belcher Islands Burwash Landing Bylot Back River Babine Buffalo Narrows

Bylot Baird Mountains Braeburn Burwash Landing Belcher Islands Babine Back River

Bb

Brenda and Billy are being chased by a bear.

Buffalo Narrows   Bear Creek   Beloud Post   Beechey Point   Banks Island   Bear Creek   Beloud Post   Beechey Point   Banks Island

Churchill   Cape Dorset   Cambridge Bay   Cumberland Sound   Coppermine   Cornwallis Island   Chesterfield Inlet   Caniapiscau   Cassiar

Chicken   Chandalar   Coffee Creek   Carcross   Camlaren   Cassiar   Chukchi Sea   Canol

Clyde River   Cambria Snowfield   Coronation Gulf   Coral Harbour   Colville Lake   Chandalar

Cc

Above the **cabin**
flies the
flag of
Canada.

Clyde River   Cambria Snowfield   Coronation Gulf   Cape Harrison   Canol   Chukchi Sea   Chicken   Camlaren   Carcross   Coffee Creek

Dd

The **ducks**
watch the
children do a
dance.

Ena River

Eden Bay

Ecklund Lake

Eagle

Ekka Island

Ellesmere Island

Eskimo Point

Ee

Eric is wearing
earmuffs.
He sees the
electric lights.

Fairbanks   Fort Smith   Fort McPherson   Faro   Frobisher Bay   Franklin   Fort Hope   Fort Liard   Forty Mile   Fullerton   Frances Lake

Fond-du-Lac   Fort Nelson   Fort Good Hope   Fort Severn   Fort Chimo   Forty Mile   Faro

Fort Collinson   Fort George   Fort Vermilion   Fort St. John   Franklin   Fort Hope   Fort Liard

Ff

The **frypan**
will soon fry
fish on the
flames.

Fort Collinson   Fort George   Fort Vermilion   Fort St. John   Fort Chimo   Fort Severn   Fort Good Hope   Fort Nelson   Fond-du-Lac

Gulkana   Gjoa Haven   Grise Fiord   Gabriel Strait   Gagnon Lake   Gardenia Lake   Garry Island   Good Point   Gordon Landing   Gakona

George River   Gods River   Goose Bay   Great Slave Lake   Great Bear Lake   Garry Island

Gg

**Georgie
is greeting
his grandmother.**

Great Bear Lake   Gods River   Grise Fiord   Gabriel Strait   Gagnon Lake   Gardenia Lake

Galena   Girdwood   Gateshead Island   Ghurka Lake   Glennallen   George River   Great Slave Lake   Goose Bay   Great Whale River

Hh

The **husky**
is watching
the boys play
hockey.

Ii

The **Inuit** children are interested in a new **igloo**.

Jj

Joe
and **Jenny**
dance a
jig.

John Richardson Bay

Jolly Lake

Joy Bay

James Bay

Jones Sound

Jackman Sound

Kk

Kate and
Kevin are
kissing behind the
kayak.

L l

The lonely **loon** floats past the **lemming.**

Mackenzie   Mount McKinley   Melville Island   Mayo   McLennan   Menihek Lakes   Manitoba   Minto   Mara River   Marsh Lake

Mansel Island

McClintock Channel

Marsh Lake

Maricourt

Mould Bay

Manitoba

Mm

Mary runs by
a **moose**
munching in the
muskeg.

MacAlpine Lake

MacInnis Lake

Maclean Strait

Manitung Island

Mara River

Mayo

MacAlpine Lake   MacInnis Lake   Maclean Strait   Maud Bight   McClure Strait   McClintock Channel   Mansel Island   Mount Logan

Nn

The **northern lights** shine in the sky at **night.**

Oo

The **owl**
can see the
oilrig from the
outhouse.

Pine Point   Pond Inlet   Pangnirtung   Povungnituk   Paulatuk   Peace River   Pelly Bay   Porcupine River   Prudhoe Bay   Point Lay

Port Radium   Port Radium   Point Barrow   Pribilof Islands   Porcupine River   Prudhoe Bay   Point Lay

Prince of Wales Island   Payne Bay   Port Harrison   Petersburg   Pelican

Pp

The man in the red
parka
is passing the
paddlewheeler.

Pribilof Islands   Prince Rupert   Port Burwell   Paxson   Pelican   Petersburg   Port Harrison   Payne Bay   Prince of Wales Island

Qq

Mother is quietly making a quilt.

Rr

Two **rabbits**
sit
outside a
root cellar.

Ss

The **sled** skims over the soft **snow.**

Tt

Trapper Tom has three frozen trout.

Uu

The constable in **uniform** likes my **uncle's** **ukulele**.

Vv

Vera takes Victor for a vaccination.

Ww

The wet **walrus** watches the **whales.**

Xx

Excited children dance round the Xmas tree.

Yy

A young
Yukoner
yells beside the
Yukon River.

Lake Hazen

Tazin Lake

Kruzof Island

Mount Edziza

Spatsizi

Rae Edzo

Elizabeth

Zz

In zero weather
Zach makes a
zigzag path to the
zinc mine.

Spatsizi

Mount Edziza

Zakwaski Mountain

Zangeza Bay

Kazan Lake

Mackenzie

Here are a few more things in the pictures that begin with each letter. Can you add still more?

A airplane… aspen trees… ax

B bark… beaver… berries… birds… black

C campfire… cap… caribou… cat… clouds

D dandelions… dog… drum… drumstick

E eagle… electricity pole… ermine… evergreen

F firewood… forest… fuel

G game… geese… gun

H hats… hockey stick… hills… horse… house

I ice… icebergs… icicles… ice floes

J jackfish… jack rabbit… jawbone… jet plane

K kerosene stove… kettle… killer whale… kindling

L ladle… lake… lamp or lantern… lightning

M magpie… mittens… moon… mountains… mukluks

N noose… nuggets (of gold)

O oildrum… orange… outboard

P pack… pail… pan

Q quills (porcupine on mukluk)

R ravens… red… ridge… rifle… river

S sky… snowshoe… spruce tree… sun

T toboggan… toque… tree

U ulu (painted on door)… underwear

V valley… veterinarian… vixen

W water… waves

X xylophone

Y yellow

Z zipper

Ted Harrison

This is the second alphabet book Ted Harrison has created. The first called NORTHLAND ALPHABET was done for the Indian and Metis children he taught at the Wabasca, Alberta, reserve a year after he came to Canada. In it he drew animals, objects and scenes that would be familiar to them.

In A NORTHERN ALPHABET he has extended the range to cover peoples living across North America, north of the 60th parallel (although in a few cases he has gone as far south as the 55th). His first book was drawn in black and white; this one is in the fabulous color that has become his trademark as an artist. It is intended for all children of the North, regardless of race or ancestry, for adults who might be learning English, and for southern children who wonder what it is like to live through the northern year.

Ted was born in England in 1926, the son of a coal-miner. He studied art and art teaching at Hartlepool and Newcastle upon Tyne. After serving with the British Intelligence Corps in Africa, the Middle East and the Far East, he returned to England. He started teaching in 1951 and taught in Malaya and New Zealand before coming to Canada.

In 1968 he accepted a teaching post in Carcross and the Yukon has been his home and inspiration ever since. It was there he discarded almost everything he had learned in formal art training and started to interpret his surroundings in a new way, so distinctive, so colorful, so magical that once seen it is unforgettable. The honors he has received and the exhibitions of his paintings stretch from Alaska down and across Canada. His first children's book CHILDREN OF THE YUKON (1977) won several awards; he was the first Canadian artist to see his work accepted into the prestigious Illustrators' Exhibit in Bologna, Italy. Another book on the Yukon, THE LAST HORIZON, followed in 1980.

He lives in Whitehorse with his wife Nicky and son Charles, both of whom helped with this alphabet book, and with Brunhilde the pup who tried to help. The increasing demand for his paintings has enabled him to retire from teaching, but he has not forgotten the children. A NORTHERN ALPHABET is for their pleasure.